INCREDIBLY DISGUSTING DRUGS

HEROIN AND YOUR VEINS
The Incredibly Disgusting Story

Allan B. Cobb

the rosen publishing group's

rosen central
new york

Published in 2000 by The Rosen Publishing Group, Inc.
29 East 21st Street, New York, NY 10010

First Edition

Library of Congress Cataloging-in-Publication Data

Cobb, Allan B.
    Heroin and your veins: the incredibly disgusting story / Allan B. Cobb.
        p. cm. — (Incredibly disgusting drugs)
    Includes bibliographical references and index.
    Summary: Discusses the illegal use of heroin as a narcotic, describing how it is taken and its physical effects on the body, especially on the veins.
    ISBN 0-8239-3249-4
    1. Heroin—Toxicology—Juvenile literature. 2. Heroin habit—Juvenile literature. [1. Heroin. 2. Drug abuse.] I. Title. II. Series.
    RA1242,H46 C63 2000
    616.86'32—dc21
                                   00-024763

Manufactured in the United States of America

CONTENTS

Introduction

Ever heard of heroin? In recent years, heroin has been showing up in the media a lot, like in the movie *Trainspotting* and among fashion models who are going for the "heroin chic" look—  superthin, pale, and kind of spaced out. But the truth is that these kinds of images are really misleading. Doing heroin isn't fashionable or cool, and it is not a form of entertainment—it is a deadly drug that has incredibly disgusting effects on your body and can definitely

Trainspotting depicts heroin use among Scottish youths.

kill you. This book gives you an up-close look at how heroin works and what it does to ruin your body and brain.

Heroin, along with opium and morphine, is in a category of drugs called narcotics. The term "narcotic" comes from the Greek work *narkosis,* which means a dazed or unconscious state. Some narcotics, like morphine, are used legally as painkillers. But others, like heroin and opium, are definitely not legal in the United States. Narcotics are among the most addictive drugs, meaning that once you start taking a narcotic, it is very hard to stop using it. The reason that narcotics are so addictive is that they are very powerful drugs that have a heavy impact on your body and brain—so heavy, in fact, that your mind and body begin to need the drug in order to function.

People use heroin for a number of reasons. One common reason people start is because they want to escape from their problems. Other people succumb to peer pressure and think it's the cool thing to do. Still others are bored and want to add excitement and danger to their lives. Whatever their reasons for taking heroin, users are setting themselves up for a vicious cycle of addiction that can last a lifetime.

For many young people, experimenting with drugs is very tempting. You see and hear about the glamorous side of drug use on television, in movies, in magazines, and in popular music all the time. Many rock stars and actors take drugs,

River Phoenix died from an overdose of heroin mixed with other drugs.

and maybe even your friends or siblings are using drugs. If people you know are doing it, it can't be that bad, right? Wrong. Keep reading to see just how bad using drugs can be.

Jan was on the soccer team, got good grades, and had lots of friends. Everything changed the day that Nikki, one of her sister's friends, offered Jan some heroin. Jan told Nikki that she wasn't a junkie and didn't want to stick a needle in her arm. Nikki told her that she didn't have to—she could just snort it.

Jan was tempted. If her sister and Nikki took heroin and they were fine, why couldn't she? Besides, she wanted to hang out more with her sister's friends, and this seemed like a great way to get in with them. So Jan gave in and tried some.

Right after taking the drug, Jan felt warm and happy all over. All of her problems seemed to melt away. She liked the feeling so much that soon she was

snorting heroin to relax after big soccer games. But then she began taking heroin before games, too, and before practice. It didn't take long for Jan's performance on the field to nosedive. She couldn't run up and down the field like before, and it was really hard for her to concentrate on making goals or playing strategy.

Her coach quickly noticed the change. She pulled Jan off the team and made her watch from the bench for the rest of the season. Jan felt embarrassed and disappointed, but she found that snorting heroin helped her forget her bad feelings.

Soon, though, the problem got much worse. Jan was spending so much time getting and snorting heroin that she wasn't hanging out with her friends anymore. The only people she saw were other heroin users. Because she knew that her friends wouldn't approve of her drug habit, Jan couldn't explain to them why she was acting weird. They just thought she was being a jerk.

Jan was getting swept up more and more into the cycle of drug abuse. To cope with all of her problems, she started snorting heroin before and after school. But that just made her grades drop, giving her yet another reason to try to escape from her problems.

After a few months, Jan realized that the drug just wasn't giving her the good feelings that it used to. Some of her sister's friends told her that she was ready for the next level—mainlining, or injecting heroin directly into her veins.

One night, at a party, Jan had a really bad reaction to heroin. She kept imagining that everyone was out to get her, and she was vomiting so much that it hurt. After that night, Jan realized just how much her drug habit was ruining her life, and she decided to quit. But quitting was worse than anything. Jan felt nauseated all the time and couldn't stop throwing up, and she had alternating hot and cold flashes. Her muscles and joints hurt. She couldn't sleep and she was irritable. She could only find relief by mainlining more heroin, but it made her sleepy, and she was scared. It was clear—she had become a junkie.

This type of story happens all the time—too many times—every day. No one starts using heroin in order to become an addict. Many people, kids and teens especially, know about the dangers of heroin and other drugs but think, "There's no way that can happen to me." The truth is that it *can* happen—to anyone, of any age, at any time.

1 What Is Heroin?

Heroin is one of many narcotics made from a plant called the opium poppy. Opium poppies have beautiful scarlet red flowers with black centers that grow on tall stalks. People began growing opium poppies and making opium from them about seven thousand years ago.

Today, opium poppies are the source of many helpful legal drugs, such as morphine, as well as many illegal and widely abused drugs. Together, all of these drugs made from the opium poppy are called opiates. Because opium poppies can be used to produce illegal drugs, it is against the law to grow opium poppies in the United States as well as many other countries around the world. Most of the world's opium supply today comes from Colombia, Mexico, Vietnam, China, Afghanistan, and Thailand.

Opium is still collected by hand from opium poppies, as it has been for thousands of years. A series of cuts are made in the unripe seedpod of the flower with a short, curved knife. A milky sap, containing opium, oozes from the cuts. Over several days, people go through the fields of poppies with burlap bags and scrape

Examining the ripe pod
of the opium poppy

the sap off the seedpods and into the burlap bags. This method of harvesting opium requires a lot of labor but is still used throughout the world. The sap that is collected is either formed into a ball called gum opium or dried and ground into a powder called opium powder, which varies in color from brown to black.

The milky sap of the opium poppy oozes out when the pod is cut open.

There's also a more modern way to extract opium from opium poppies: the industrial poppy straw process. In this method, dried opium poppy plants are harvested and ground up, and the opium is extracted. The result is a fine brownish powder called poppy straw concentrate. Poppy straw concentrate is the starting point for the legal manufacture of many different opium-based drugs, such as morphine and codeine. Each year, about 500 tons of opium straw concentrate are imported into the United States for use in the pharmaceutical industry.

THE HISTORY OF HEROIN

Opium was legally imported into the United States until the early 1900s. It was a common ingredient in cough medicines and other products. In the mid- to late 1800s, opium dens, introduced by immigrants from Asia, became increasingly popular in America. Opium dens were dark and dirty places where people smoked opium and laid about in a semiconscious state. Surveys conducted between 1878 and 1885 showed that about 5 out of every 1,000 Americans were opium addicts. (Today, it is estimated that only about 2 out of every 1,000 Americans are addicted to opium.) These surveys shocked the nation, and the U.S. government began searching for ways to prevent opium addiction. Laws were passed greatly restricting the use of opium. Eventually, the use of opium was banned, and importing opium into the United States was declared illegal.

Research into opium and its effects led to the discovery of morphine in 1803. Morphine was named for Morpheus, the Greek god of dreams. The commercial production of morphine began in 1823. Morphine was, and still is, used as a powerful legal painkiller for people who are in severe pain due to illness or injury. Although morphine is an extremely effective painkiller, it is highly addictive. Users quickly develop a tolerance to it, meaning that over time, they need larger and larger doses of the drug to get the same effect.

A substance called diacetylmorphine was discovered in 1874 as a result of attempts to make a less addictive but still effective painkiller. Heroin is the common name for diacetylmorphine, which is made from morphine through a chemical process. Unfortunately, researchers soon discovered that heroin was even more addictive than the morphine it was supposed to replace. As a result, medical professionals did not use heroin as a medical painkiller for long. It soon became popular as a drug of abuse, however.

STREET HEROIN

Street heroin varies greatly in purity and strength, making it extremely dangerous.

Heroin sold on the street today is also made from morphine, but dealers add other materials to make it go farther. Street heroin varies in color from white to brown, depending on its impurities and the substances added to it. This means that like most street drugs, heroin sold on the street is rarely pure. You never really know what you are getting when you buy off the street.

A bag, or single dose of heroin, usually contains about 100 milligrams of powder. This powder can range from about 1 to 98 percent heroin—35 percent is average. The rest of the powder is made up of additives such as sugar, starch, powdered milk, talcum powder, and quinine. The additives are mixed with the heroin to "cut," or dilute, the heroin so that the dealer will make more money selling it.

Another common form of street heroin, called black-tar heroin, is dark brown or black in color and is either sticky like tar or formed into hard lumps like coal. It usually contains 20 to 80 percent heroin. Like heroin powder, black-tar heroin has many different impurities and additives. Most black-tar heroin is illegally produced in Mexico and then smuggled into the United States.

The heroin sold on the street today is usually much stronger and more dangerous than what was available ten years ago. As a result, heroin users today take in much more heroin each time they snort, smoke, or inject it. And that means that heroin users today are at a much greater risk of overdosing on heroin.

2 How Is Heroin Used?

Most users take heroin by mainlining, or injecting the drug into their veins with a syringe. Ugly scars on the forearm are a sign of mainlining. Heroin can also be injected into a muscle or just under the skin. This also causes scarring, as well as infection.

SNIFFING, SNORTING, AND SMOKING

As you know, users can also sniff or snort heroin. This method

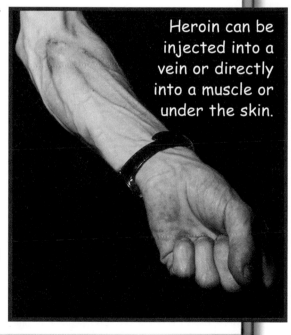

Heroin can be injected into a vein or directly into a muscle or under the skin.

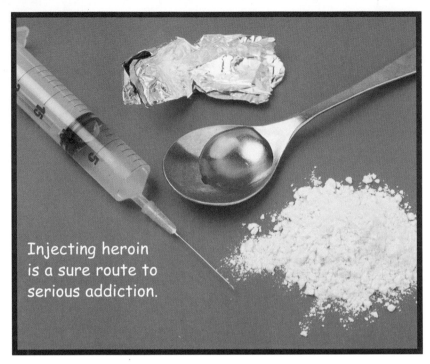

Injecting heroin is a sure route to serious addiction.

has become much more popular, especially in wealthy and chic crowds. Since heroin that is snorted takes longer to have an effect than injected heroin, very pure, expensive forms of the drug are needed for snorting to work.

Heroin can also be smoked in a pipe or snorted in a nasal inhaler. Heroin users often use other drugs along with heroin. These drugs include alcohol, marijuana, cocaine, crack, and tranquilizers and other "downers." Some users alternate doses of heroin and cocaine, which is called crisscrossing, or inject a mixture of cocaine and heroin. Bored with the effects of heroin, users crave new combinations of drugs to avoid depression, but these combinations have unpredictable and dangerous effects on the body.

WHAT'S THE RUSH?

All of these methods are used to get a rush or high. If heroin is injected into a vein, the rush begins quickly. If the drug is smoked or snorted, the rush takes longer to kick in. A heroin rush begins as a warm feeling in the skin. Users generally feel some other, less pleasant effects right away, like dry mouth, watery eyes and runny nose, constricted (narrowed) pupils, and a heavy feeling in the arms and legs.

Then the user experiences nausea, vomiting, and severe itching. These symptoms gradually change into a trancelike state, in which your awareness seems to fade away. These feelings are then replaced with a feeling of deep drowsiness or sleepiness, mental stupor, and slowed breathing and heartbeat. Overall, regardless of the method used, a heroin rush may last for four to six hours.

THE ROAD TO ADDICTION

Most heroin users don't begin by injecting the drug. They usually start out as occasional or recreational users, called chippers, not understanding where they may be headed. Chippers usually sniff, smoke, or inhale their heroin. After a while, however, they find that they are no

17

longer getting the highs that they used to. To increase the rush from heroin, they try injecting heroin under their skin. Soon even this doesn't give enough of a rush, so users often graduate to mainlining, or injecting heroin directly into their veins. At this point, the user is psychologically and physically addicted to heroin.

Occasional users do not think that they are addicted to heroin or even dependent on it. They may continue their occasional use for months or even years, fooling themselves about their dependence. During this time, they are building up a tolerance for heroin. Each time they use heroin, it takes a little more of the drug to get the same feeling.

HOW IS HEROIN TAKEN?

To snort heroin, the user draws the heroin directly into the nostril. Smoking heroin involves placing the heroin in a pipe, lighting it, and then inhaling the smoke.

Injecting, or shooting up, heroin involves mixing water and heroin and injecting the mixture into a vein. But if the needle misses the vein or goes through it, something pretty disgusting happens: The user gets a painful blister. Even if done properly, over time ugly scars

Injecting heroin is very dangerous. Fatal overdoses are common.

will form near the site of the injections, and the veins will collapse.

There is no mistaking a heroin addict when you see where that person has injected needles repeatedly into his or her skin. An addict will often try to conceal his or her habit from others by injecting heroin into parts of the body that people don't usually see, such as the back of the knee.

3 What Happens Inside Your Body?

Heroin affects the body's central nervous system, including the brain. But how does heroin get to your brain if it is injected into your veins or inhaled into your nose? The answer is through the circulatory system—the heart and the blood vessels, which are tubes that carry blood through your body. The circulatory system is part of a larger system called the cardiovascular system, which also includes the lungs.

Blood is a liquid that is mostly made up of water. Blood also contains salts, red blood cells, white blood cells, nutrients, and wastes. Red blood cells carry oxygen to all the cells in the body and carry away cellular waste and carbon dioxide. In addition, blood carries nutrients that cells need in order to survive.

The Circulatory System

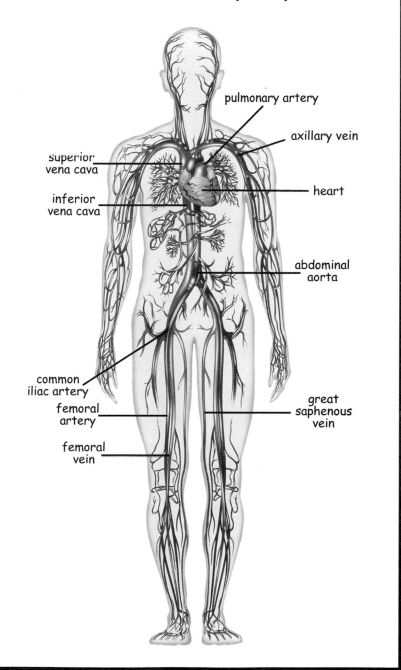

pulmonary artery

axillary vein

superior vena cava

inferior vena cava

heart

abdominal aorta

common iliac artery

femoral artery

femoral vein

great saphenous vein

THE CIRCULATORY SYSTEM

The circulatory system is made up of the heart and all the veins, arteries, and capillaries through which blood travels. The human heart is a big muscle with four chambers separated from each other by valves. The valves prevent blood from flowing backward through the system between contractions (movements) of the heart muscles. Blood from your body first enters a chamber called the right atrium. As your heart muscles contract, blood is squeezed from the right atrium through a valve and into the right ventricle. The contractions in the heart muscle then force the blood out of the right ventricle and into the pulmonary artery, through which blood flows to the lungs.

When blood reaches your lungs, it flows through the pulmonary artery and then into smaller and smaller vessels in the lungs until it reaches tiny ones called capillaries. Capillaries are thin-walled blood vessels

capillary

Capillaries are small blood vessels that connect arteries and veins, allowing blood to flow throughout the body.

Diagram of the Heart

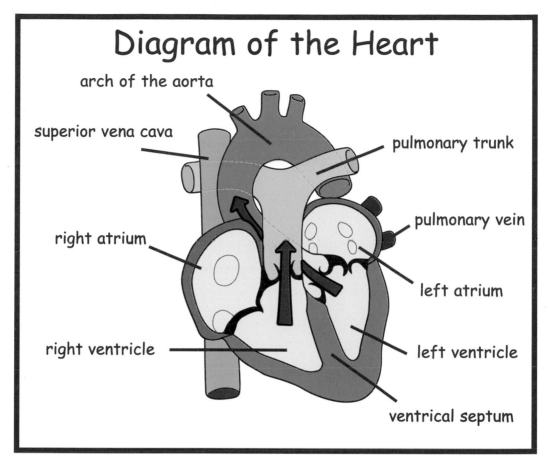

arch of the aorta

superior vena cava

pulmonary trunk

pulmonary vein

right atrium

left atrium

right ventricle

left ventricle

ventrical septum

that are about the same size in diameter as a red blood
cell. On the surface of the lung's capillaries are structures
called alveoli. This is where the gases in the blood are
exchanged. The carbon dioxide in the blood is passed into
the lungs and is then breathed out into the air. At the
same time, oxygen in the lungs is picked up by red blood
cells, which carry the gas to other cells in your body.

After the blood cells pick up oxygen and release their
carbon dioxide, they flow from the capillaries into larger

vessels called veins. The veins come together into the large pulmonary vein, which enters the heart at the left atrium. From the left atrium, the blood then flows into the left ventricle, where a powerful pump sends the blood into the arteries.

Arteries typically have thick walls because they have to be strong enough to carry blood under high pressure. The arteries branch into smaller and smaller arteries and then into very small capillaries. When blood flows through the capillaries, it comes into direct contact with cells. Every cell in the body is in direct contact with a capillary. When the blood reaches a cell, red blood cells pass oxygen to that cell. Nutrients in the blood are also passed to the cells.

At the same time, these cells release carbon dioxide and wastes, which are absorbed by the capillaries and passed into the veins. Veins typically have thinner walls than arteries because the blood is no longer at a high pressure. Some larger veins have valves of their own to keep blood from flowing backward. On the way back to the heart, the veins pass through the liver and kidneys, which filter waste products out of the blood. Eventually, all the veins come together and reach the heart. The blood enters the heart at the right atrium, and the whole process begins again.

The average adult male has about 5.5 quarts of blood in his body, and the average adult female has about 3.5 quarts of blood. The heart rate of an average adult is about seventy-five beats per minute. Each heartbeat pumps about 2.5 ounces of blood into the body. During the course of a day, the heart pumps about 2,500 gallons of blood. This means that the blood is circulated through the body about 500 times every day!

HEROIN AND THE BLOODSTREAM

When heroin is inhaled or snorted, it is absorbed through the sinuses—hollow passages connected to the nose and mouth—and enters the bloodstream. This process is pretty slow because the heroin must pass through the membranes in the nasal passage before it enters the blood. Once it enters the bloodstream, the drug passes through the circulatory system until it reaches the brain. Injecting heroin under the skin produces faster effects than snorting because the heroin enters the bloodstream directly.

As mentioned in the last chapter, even people who start out snorting often eventually begin to mainline in order to get this faster effect. But controlling the dosage is much more difficult this way, and the dangers of a lethal overdose or some frightening reaction are much greater.

4 How Does Heroin Affect Your Body?

Heroin affects your body as soon as it enters the bloodstream. The speed at which heroin affects your body depends on the method of taking it. When heroin is injected directly into a vein, you feel the effects very quickly—in about seven or eight seconds. When heroin is snorted, it has to pass through the membranes in the nasal passages before it enters the bloodstream, which takes about ten to fifteen minutes. That's why it takes longer for the user to feel the rush when snorting heroin. Smoking heroin has a slightly quicker effect than snorting it because the smoke crosses into the bloodstream through the lungs.

Heroin affects many systems in the body.

Once heroin enters your bloodstream, it quickly passes through the circulatory system to other systems throughout the body. Heroin affects the central nervous system (the brain and nerves), respiratory system (lungs and breathing), the digestive and excretory system, the reproductive and endocrine (hormonal) systems, the skin, and the circulatory system.

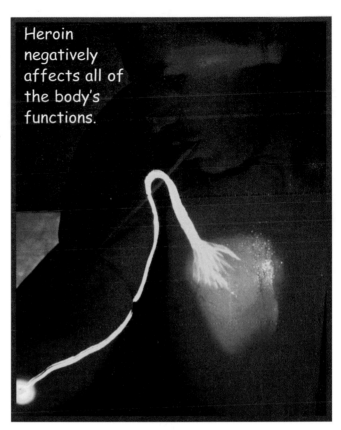

Heroin negatively affects all of the body's functions.

HEROIN AND THE BRAIN

The euphoria that goes along with the rush is a result of the effects of heroin on the central nervous system. The central nervous system is made up of the brain, the spinal column, and the main nerves throughout the body.

This system is responsible for sending nerve signals from the body to the brain and vice versa.

Exactly how heroin affects the brain was not understood until 1974. Scientists discovered that the brain and other parts of the central nervous system have special receptors—cells that receive signals from the brain—to which heroin binds. The way that these receptor sites work can be thought of as a lock and key. The receptor site is the lock. To "unlock" the receptor site, a molecule has to be a certain shape. A molecule of the right shape acts like a key and unlocks the site. Not just any key can unlock the receptor site. It takes a particular molecular pattern to bind to the receptor site and unlock it.

Once the receptor site is "unlocked," it responds in a particular way. When the molecules in heroin and related drugs bind to these sites, a trancelike stupor floods your body. Heroin also causes extreme sleepiness. Another effect is that the pupils of the eyes constrict, or narrow.

The Role of Endorphins

Why do humans—and all other animals with backbones—have these receptor sites for heroin-like drugs in their brains? The answer to this question was discovered in 1975. The brain's pituitary gland, which watches over many functions of the body, produces its own substances that are shaped similarly to opiates. These substances are called endorphins. The structure of the molecules in opiates is similar enough to that of the molecules in endorphins that they can bind to the same receptor sites in the brain.

Endorphins, the body's natural analgesics (painkillers), produce pleasurable and safe effects similar to those of narcotic drugs.

Endorphins are the body's natural painkillers. They allow the body to endure stress and pain. When the body is injured, endorphins are released to protect the body. Endorphins are also released during exercise, leading to the "runner's high" or "endorphin rush" that runners and other athletes often experience.

HEROIN AND YOUR CIRCULATORY SYSTEM

As the circulatory system carries heroin throughout the body, the heroin gradually causes your blood pressure to drop and lowers your heart rate slightly. Because of the drop in blood pressure, many heroin users faint when they try to stand after shooting up. This happens because blood can't reach the brain fast enough after such a sudden movement. This also makes the user lethargic and dull-witted because not enough oxygen is reaching the brain.

Different substances have different effects on your blood vessels. Some cause them to constrict, or tighten up, which makes it more difficult for blood to flow through them. Heroin does the opposite: It makes the blood vessels widen, which temporarily makes blood flow more freely through the body. This helps create the relaxed feeling that heroin users experience right after the drug enters their bloodstream.

Long-term heroin use can do serious—and pretty dis-gusting—damage to the veins and heart. People who take heroin by mainlining damage their veins at the sites of injec-tion. Your veins can become so weak that they collapse and become completely unusable. If that happens, the areas of your body that aren't receiving blood anymore are no longer alive. These areas become discolored and infected, and are truly repulsive to look at. Eventually, they become dead and will need to be amputated—gross!

Veins can also get so scarred that it becomes impossible to inject heroin into them anymore. When this happens, junkies tend to start using other veins located in the hands, legs, and feet. After years of heroin use, heroin users may have difficulty finding a vein to inject into! One sure sign of a junkie is track marks—the scars from repeated injections on the arms and legs. Collapsed and scarred veins can cause long-lasting problems, even if the junkie eventually kicks the heroin habit. The person will always have poor circulation and can easily develop circulatory diseases.

Here's another really serious danger of taking heroin: If junkies use dirty needles, their veins can become infected. These infections can spread all over the body and can cause serious damage to vital parts of the body, including the heart, liver, and kidneys. In addition, if heroin users share needles, they are at risk of getting certain diseases that other people who used the needle have. These include hepatitis B and C, which are serious diseases of the liver,

Hepatitis, or inflammation of the liver, can easily be contracted through the use of a dirty needle.

and HIV, the deadly virus that causes AIDS. You may have heard about the importance of lowering the amount of fat in your diet. This is because diets that are high in fats can clog arteries. Guess what? Some of the substances that are added to heroin can cause clogging of the blood vessels, too. So can bacteria that may enter the bloodstream along with heroin when the drug is injected. When blood vessels become clogged, the heart has to pump harder to push blood through the body. This puts a lot of strain on your heart and can weaken it.

Long-term heroin users have a much greater risk than

nonusers of developing a serious heart disease called subacute bacterial endocarditis (SBE). This is an infection of the lining of the heart. It is caused by bacteria that enter the blood-stream. SBE can be treated with medica-tion or surgery, but because heroin addicts do not usually see doctors regularly or take good care of themselves, they may have SBE without knowing it. If left untreated, SBE can cause permanent heart damage and even death.

Endocarditis, or inflammation of the lining of the heart cavity, can result in hemor-rhage, or bleeding, of the body's delicate membranes, such as those in the eyes.

Because your veins are connected to your heart, any-thing that you put in your veins will also reach your heart. Some substances, including pure heroin in large doses, can make your heart stop pumping. Know what that means? If your heart isn't pumping blood to your body, you will die. Your veins are small, but they are an important part of your

endocarditis

Here, endocarditis has caused infection to the heart valve. This can be only treated with antibiotic drugs.

circulatory system. Keeping your veins clean and healthy is necessary to keep your heart functioning well—and to keep you alive.

HEROIN AND YOUR BODY

Heroin has strong effects on the digestive and excretory systems, which are the systems that process and get rid of the food you eat. Heroin causes the muscles in your intestines to stiffen. When the muscles become rigid, the motion that pushes food and waste through the intestines stops. This causes constipation. In fact, one of the legal medical uses of opiates is to control diarrhea. Heroin also affects the muscles in the bladder, causing them to stiffen, too. This causes difficult and painful urination. These effects can last for days, even after a single dose of heroin.

Heroin also acts to decrease your appetite. This is caused partly by the stopped motion of the digestive system. As a result, serious heroin users often suffer from poor nutrition. They also feel nauseated and vomit frequently.

Heroin use causes your skin to feel flushed and warm, and also makes you sweaty and itchy. Addicts can judge the strength of a dose of heroin by how it makes their skin feel. Some dealers cut heroin with quinine, a bitter-tasting drug that, when injected, makes the skin flush and feel itchy.

ADDICTION

Heroin is extremely physically addictive. Once the body is exposed to opium and its derivatives, the brain tells the body that it needs the drug to survive. When the brain becomes dependent on opiates such as heroin, it tells the body that it needs more. To convince the body to give the brain more opiates, the brain starts causing withdrawal symptoms. Symptoms of withdrawal include sleeplessness, watery eyes, yawning, muscle aches and spasms, joint pain, vomiting, diarrhea, alternating hot and cold flashes, anxiety, and hostile behavior. Although many of these early symptoms of withdrawal pass in a few days, the cravings and some of the symptoms can last for several months. Without treatment, these withdrawal symptoms are usually so unpleasant and painful that they make the user seek out more heroin.

Casual or one-time heroin users may tell you that they don't feel the effects of addiction and withdrawal, but that's only because the effects are mild at first. The truth is, heroin addiction begins with the first use. As tolerance develops and the user takes more and more heroin, the brain becomes more addicted. And as the addiction increases, so does the severity of the withdrawal symptoms.

5 How Is Heroin Addiction Treated?

Even casual or recreational users experience heroin withdrawal symptoms, usually as a run-down feeling or flulike symptoms that pass within a day or so. With continued use, however, a tolerance to heroin develops. As tolerance grows, more heroin must be used to get a rush. As you become more and more addicted to heroin, the withdrawal symptoms that you will experience if you try to quit become increasingly serious. In heavy heroin users, the withdrawal symptoms become extremely severe. They crave another dose, or fix, so badly that they'll do whatever it takes to get more heroin.

For serious users, withdrawal symptoms peak twenty-four to forty-eight hours after their last fix. The symptoms include muscle aches, sleeplessness, watery eyes, joint pain, vomiting, diarrhea, yawning, anxiety, alternating hot and cold flashes, and hostile behavior. Without another fix, heroin users can feel these symptoms for months.

Heroin withdrawal produces nightmarish feelings.

EXPENSIVE TASTE

Junkies usually need to shoot up every two to six hours. That makes for a pretty expensive habit—like $100 to $200 every day. To raise this much money daily, junkies often turn to crime. Some become dealers to support their habit. As their drug habit gets worse, they sell less and less of their stash to customers and keep more and more of it for themselves. Most heroin addicts turn to stealing, shoplifting, robbery, or prostitution to support their habit.

Heroin users may also eventually suffer from an overdose, which means that the level of heroin in the body is too high. When users buy drugs on the street, they don't know what they are buying. If they buy heroin that is much stronger than what they are used to, it's easy for them to take too much without knowing it.

OVERDOSING

An overdose of heroin can lead to death within minutes of injection by causing breathing to stop. Even if it doesn't cause breathing to stop completely, an overdose of heroin can slow down breathing so much that it leads to a coma. People who have overdosed on heroin are usually treated with the injection of a drug that blocks heroin from binding to receptor sites in the central nervous system.

FROM USER TO ADDICT

So when does a user become an addict? Obviously, someone who is shooting up heroin every few hours is definitely an addict. But what about the casual or recreational user? Well, here's the scary truth: Anyone who has used heroin—even just once—is addicted. Even after a person takes heroin for the first time, his or her brain begins to crave heroin, and even if the withdrawal symptoms are very mild, they still occur.

TREATMENT

Treating occasional or recreational users is usually easy. Because the withdrawal symptoms are mild, they pass quickly. The addiction cycle is easily broken through education, involvement in support groups, and simply staying away from heroin. With addicts, however, treating addiction is extremely difficult. Many addicts in treatment take a drug called methadone to help them kick their heroin habit. Addicts who don't use methadone go "cold turkey," meaning that they completely stop taking heroin. Going cold turkey is really, really difficult because the cravings for heroin are extremely strong. For this reason, most addicts are not successful going cold turkey. Although people in withdrawal often feel like they are going to die if they don't take more heroin, the symptoms of withdrawal are not fatal.

Methadone

Here's how methadone works. Methadone is a synthetic (man-made) version of morphine that has many of the same effects as morphine and heroin. Like these other drugs, methadone is addictive. The advantage of methadone, however, is that unlike heroin, methadone is taken orally (by mouth). This means that methadone is absorbed into the bloodstream through the intestines, which takes much more time than absorption through the veins, nose, or lungs. Because of the slow absorption, there is no rush associated with taking methadone. This means that methadone is useful in treating heroin addiction because it prevents the body from suffering withdrawal symptoms. It also reduces the risk of disease and infection from using dirty or infected needles.

When heroin addicts enter a methadone treatment program, they attend support group meetings where they share their experiences and concerns with other recovering addicts. This helps addicts feel as though they are not alone. They also receive counseling to help them overcome their addictive behaviors.

Patients start taking methadone right away and continue to take it for months. Toward the end of treatment, the doctor begins decreasing the dose in order to slowly end the methadone addiction. Heroin addiction is often successfully treated with methadone, especially when the patient has a strong desire to break the addiction cycle.

If you or a friend needs help overcoming a drug problem, help is available. Family, friends, and religious groups can provide support and help locate treatment centers. In addition, there are plenty of drug abuse hotlines that you can call for advice and support. Some of these hotlines are listed in the back of this book, and you can find others in phone books, in antidrug pamphlets, and on antidrug posters and television commercials.

In addition, most states have commissions on drug and alcohol abuse that help addicts find treatment programs. Hospitals and doctors' offices have information on area treatment and rehabilitation centers. Finding help for addiction is easy. The difficult part is admitting that you or a friend has a problem.

GLOSSARY

endorphin   A substance produced by the pituitary gland similar in structure to opiates. Endorphins act as natural painkillers.

intravenous   An injection directly into a vein.

methadone   Synthetic opiate used in the treatment of heroin addiction.

morphine   A natural component of opium that is used as a painkiller.

narcotic   A substance that causes sleepiness.

opiates   Drugs such as morphine and heroin that are derived, or made from, the opium poppy.

track marks   Marks and scars on the skin from veins damaged as a result of injecting heroin.

FOR MORE INFORMATION

Center for Substance Abuse Prevention (CSAP)
http://www.samhsa.gov/csap

Community Anti-Drug Coalition of America
http://www.cadca.org

DEAL: Drug Education and Awareness for Life (Canada)
http://www.deal.org/english

Narcotics Anonymous Canada
http://www.na.org

National Clearinghouse for Alcohol and Drug Information
http://www.health.org

National Institute on Drug Abuse
http://www.nida.nih.gov

National Youth Anti-Drug Media Campaign
http://www.mediacampaign.org

Partnership for a Drug-Free America
http://www.drugfreeamerica.org

FOR FURTHER READING

Burgess, Melvin. *Smack.* New York: Henry Holt & Co., 1998.

DeStefano, Susan. *Focus on Opiates.* New York: Twenty-First Century Books, 1995.

Fernandez, Humberto. *Heroin.* Center City, MN: Hazelden Foundation, 1998.

Glass, George. *Narcotics: Dangerous Painkillers.* New York: Rosen Publishing Group, 1998.

Kirby-Payne, Ann. *Refuse to Use: A Girl's Guide to Drugs and Alcohol.* New York: Rosen Publishing Group, 1999.

Mass, Wendy. *Teen Drug Abuse.* San Diego, CA: Lucent Books, 1997.

McLaughlin, Miriam Smith, and Sandra Peyser Hazouri. *Addiction: The "High" That Brings You Down.* Springfield, NJ: Enslow Publishers, 1997.

Smith, Sandra Lee. *Heroin.* New York: Rosen Publishing Group, 1995.

Woods, Geraldine. *Heroin.* Springfield, NJ: Enslow Publishers, 1994.

INDEX

CREDITS

About the Author

Allan Cobb is a freelance science writer living in central Texas. He has written books, radio scripts, articles, and educational materials concerning different aspects of science. He also enjoys traveling, camping, hiking, and exploring caves.

Photo Credits

Series and Layout Design

Laura Murawski